D1281504

Tail Toes Eyes Ears Nose

by Marilee Robin Burton

HarperCollins*Publishers*

With special thanks to Jerry Jarvis

Tail Toes Eyes Ears Nose
Copyright © 1988 by Marilee Robin Burton
All rights reserved. No part of this book may be used or
reproduced in any manner whatsoever without written permission
except in the case of brief quotations embodied in critical articles
and reviews. Printed in Mexico. For information address
HarperCollins Children's Books, a division of HarperCollins
Publishers, 10 East 53rd Street, New York, NY 10022.

Library of Congress Cataloging-in-Publication Data
Burton, Marilee Robin.
  Tail, toes, eyes, ears, nose / by Marilee Robin Burton.—1st ed.
    p.   cm.
  Summary: Presents body parts of eight animals for the reader to
guess what the whole animal looks like.
    ISBN 0-06-020873-2.—ISBN 0-06-020874-0 (lib. bdg.)
    ISBN 0-06-443260-2 (pbk.)
    1. Animals—Pictorial works—Juvenile literature.   2. Morphology
(Animals)—Pictorial works—Juvenile literature.   3. Picture
puzzles—Juvenile literature.   [1. Animals—Pictorial works.
2. Morphology (Animals)—Pictorial works.   3. Picture puzzles.]
I. Title.
QL49.B796   1988   87-33276
E—dc19   CIP
                                                          AC

Typography by Andrew Rhodes

For My Mother

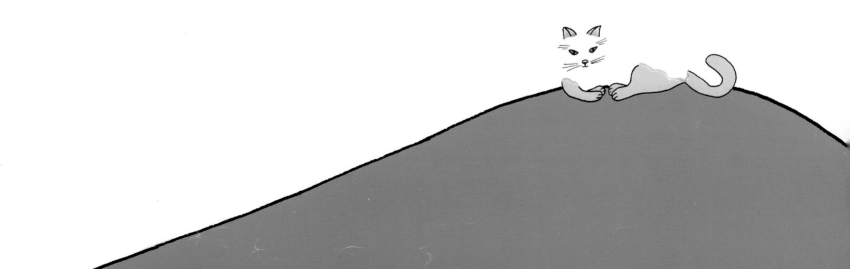

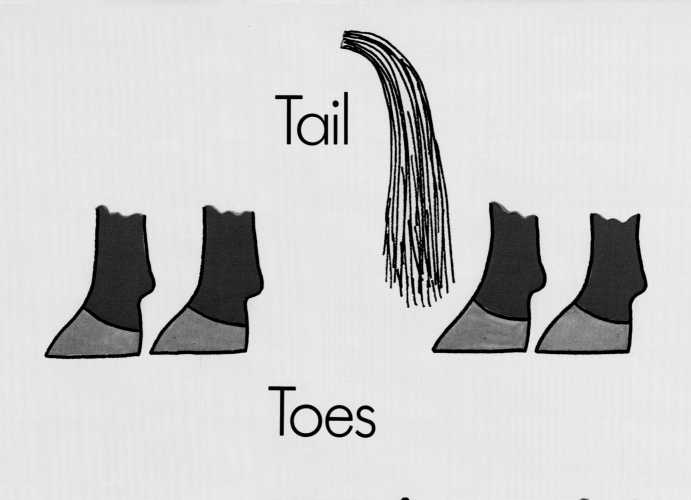

Tail

Toes

Eyes

Ears

Nose

Horse

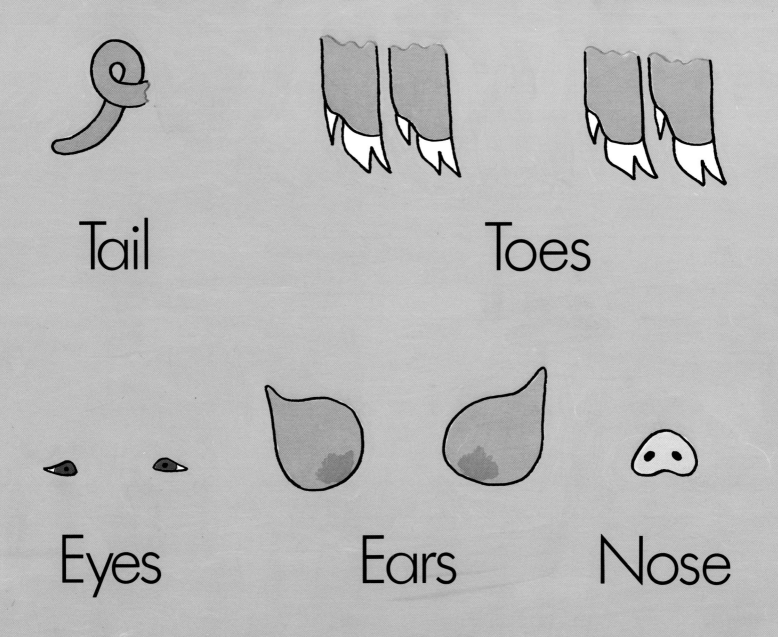

Tail

Toes

Eyes

Ears

Nose

Pig

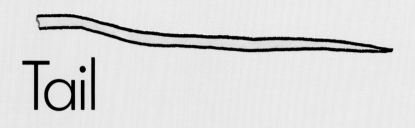

Tail

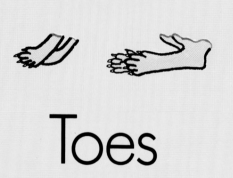 

Toes

Eyes

Ears

Nose

Mouse

Tail

Toes   Eyes   Ears   Nose

Cat

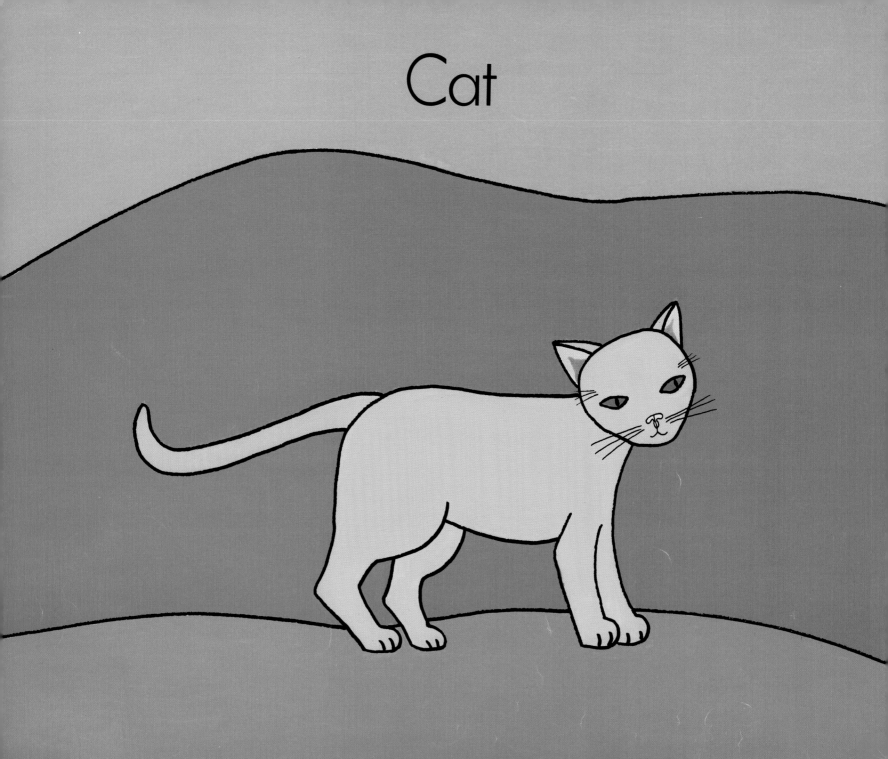

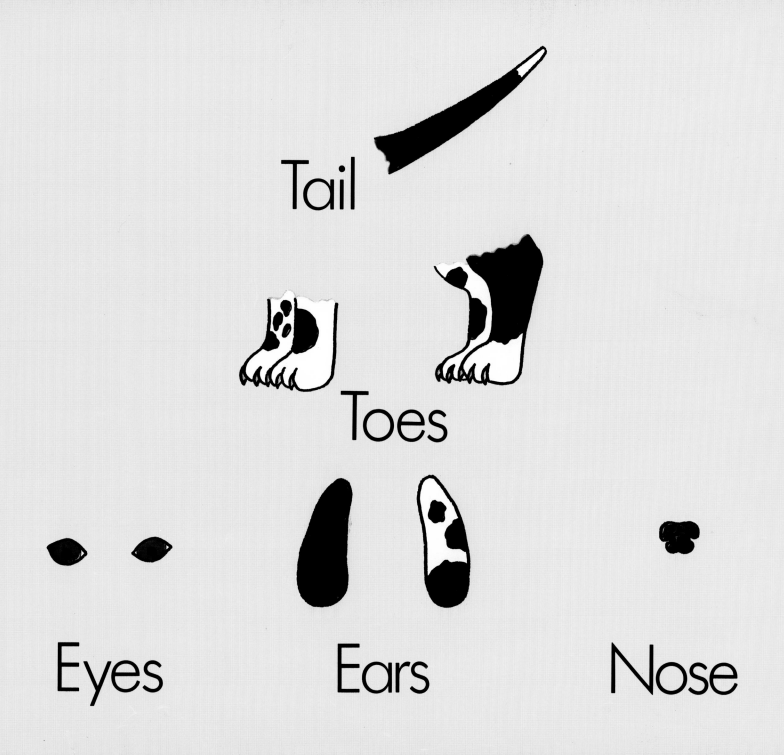

Tail

Toes

Eyes   Ears   Nose

Dog

Tail

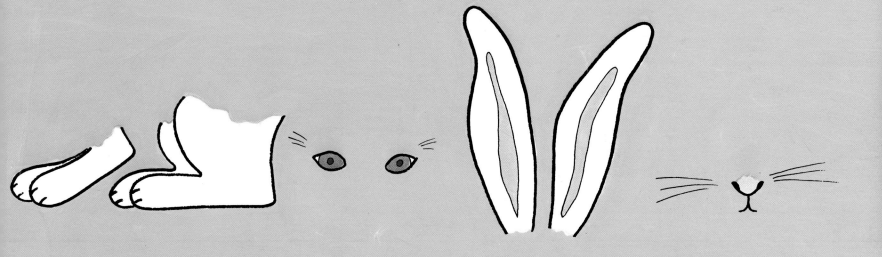

Toes   Eyes   Ears   Nose

Rabbit

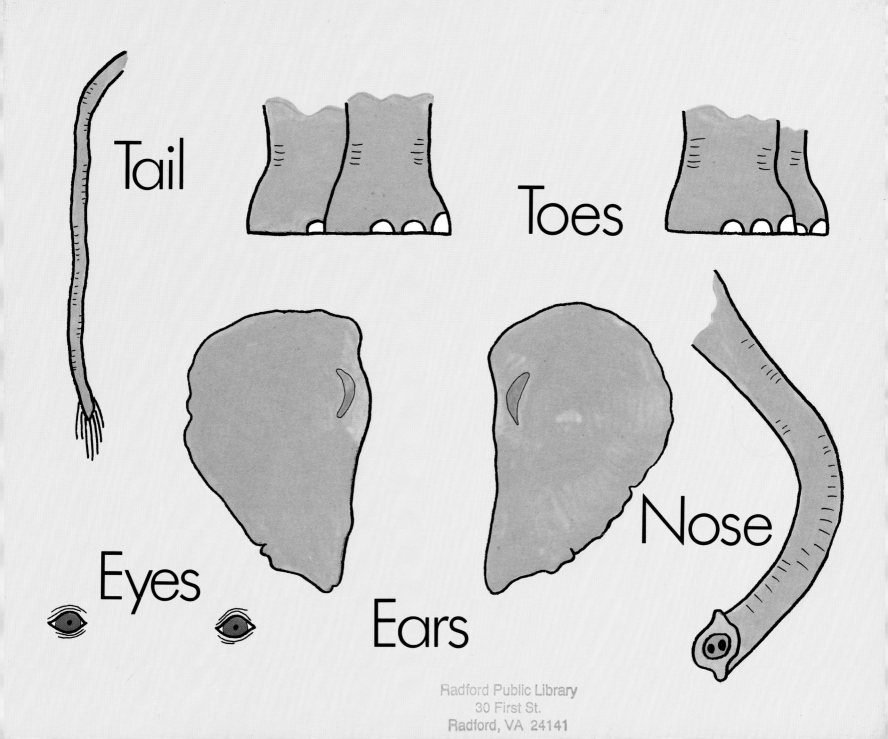

Tail

Toes

Eyes

Ears

Nose

Elephant

Tail   Toes   Eyes   Ears   Nose

(hidden)

Bird

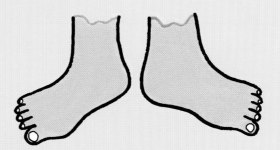

Tail

Toes

Eyes

Ears

Nose

Person

Tails

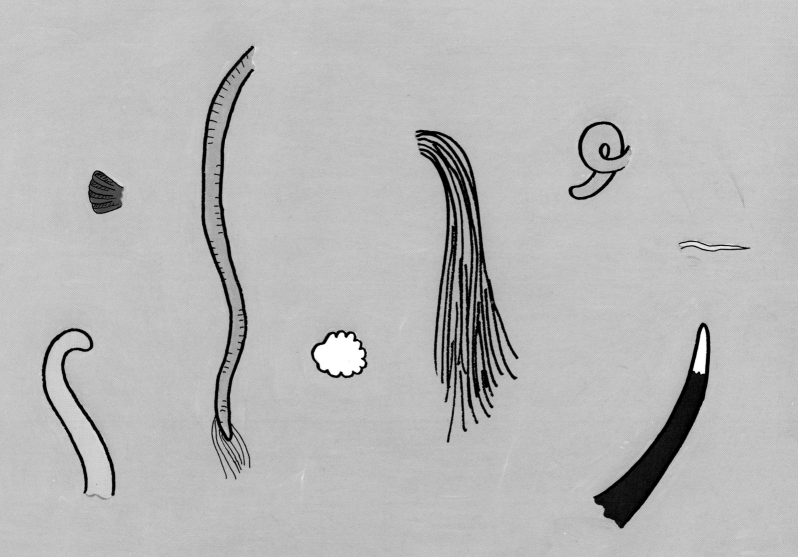

Toes

Eyes

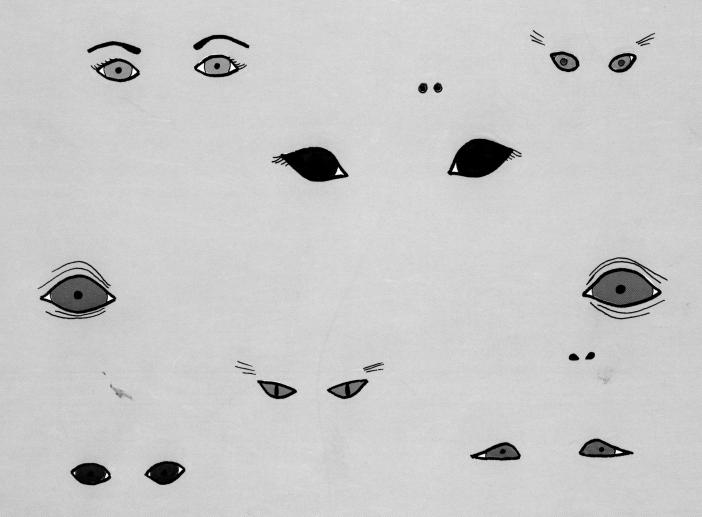

Ears

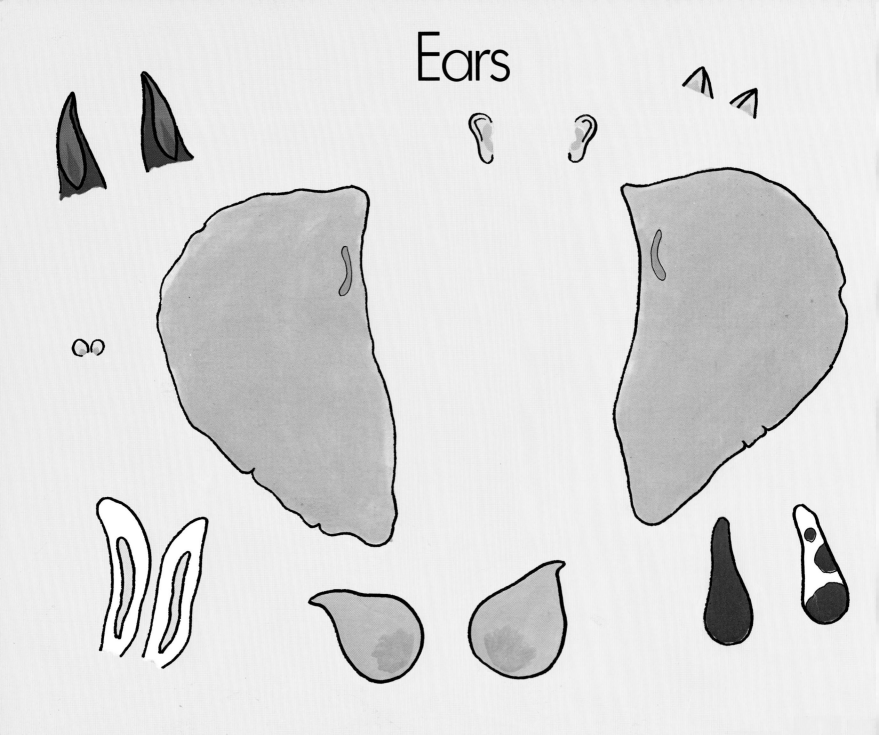

Noses